Presented to

_____

On the occasion of

_____

From

_____

Date

_____

© MCMXCVI by Barbour Publishing, Inc.

ISBN 1-55748-780-4

All Scripture quotations marked KJV are taken from The Authorized King James Version.

All Scripture quotations marked NIV are taken from the HOLY BIBLE, NEW INTERNATIONAL VERSION®. NIV®. Copyright © 1973, 1978, 1984 by International Bible Society. Used by permission of Zondervan Publishing House. All rights reserved.

Published by Barbour Publishing, Inc.
        P.O. Box 719
        Uhrichsville, Ohio 44683
        http://www.barbourbooks.com

 Member of the
Evangelical Christian
Publishers Association

Printed in the United States of America.

APPLES for A TEACHER

Colleen L. Reece
Anita Corrine Donihue

BARBOUR
PUBLISHING, INC.
Uhrichsville, Ohio

WHAT MATTERS

Some rely on stocks and bonds
In order to gain security.
Others invest in children's lives
And are builders for eternity.

Father, keep me focused on what really matters.

ONE OF THE LEAST OF THESE

"Then shall the righteous answer him, saying, Lord, when saw we thee an hungred, and fed thee? or thirsty, and gave thee drink? When saw we thee a stranger, and took thee in? or naked, and clothed thee? Or when saw we thee sick, or in prison, and came unto thee?

"And the King shall answer and say unto them, Verily I say unto you, Inasmuch as ye have done it unto one of the least of these my brethren, ye have done it unto me."

MATTHEW 25:37-40, KJV

A BAR OF SOAP

Fourth-grader Tommy always came to school dirty and unkempt. His face and hands were grimy. Even his socks gave off a bad odor. His parents obviously didn't take care of him.

One day Tommy's teacher called him to her desk. "Do you want to feel better about yourself?"

Tommy nodded shyly.

Mrs. Skylar gave him a bar of soap. "When I look good, I feel good, too," she told him. "When you run out of soap, let me know and I'll give you a new bar." She smiled.

Tommy gradually took on a cleaner appearance. He even washed his own socks! Best of all, he found a pride and a confidence he had never before known.

Lord, cleanse me inside as well as out.

PARENT-TEACHER CONFERENCE

Miss Garland dreaded her last conference of the day. One particular father never cooperated with her suggestions and always acted angry and defensive. She could see his attitude being duplicated in his seven-year-old daughter, Chelsie.

The teacher prayed for guidance. Chelsie's father arrived. Without prompting, he poured out emotions from a broken heart. His wife had died of cancer the year before. Without family in the area, he was trying to raise Chelsie as best he could.

God nudged Miss Garland and gave her a tender, listening heart. A bond formed as teacher and parent agreed to work together for a common goal: Chelsie.

Father, help me to recognize the needs and hurts of parents as well as those of the children You have given into my charge.

...the LORD said to Samuel, "Do not consider his appearance or his height...Man looks at the outward appearance, but the Lord looks at the heart." 1 SAMUEL 16:7, NIV

THE TONE OF VOICE

It's not so much what we say
As the manner in which we say it.
It's not so much the language we use
As the tone in which we convey it.

"Come here!" I sharply ordered;
And a child cowered and wept.
"Come here," I softly whispered;
And into my arms he crept.

Words may be mild and fair,
But the tone pierces like a dart.
Words may be soft as summer air,
But the tone can break a heart.

AUTHOR UNKNOWN

MISGUIDED MISSILE

Sandra McDonald's head pounded. Report card time—how she hated it! Just then a paper airplane whizzed past her head.

"Anthony, come here this instant!" she ordered, crumpling the guided missile.

"But, Miss McDonald—"

"Don't 'Miss McDonald' me." She sternly pointed to the corner. Anthony's head drooped, and he shuffled to obey.

Jake raised his hand. "Please, Miss McDonald. Open the airplane."

Sighing with frustration but unable to resist his pleading expression, Miss McDonald complied. Her eyes stung when she read, "We love you." Every student had signed it.

"Anthony, I'm sorry. Forgive me?"

"Sure, Miss McDonald. You look tired, and we just wanted to help."

"You did. You'll never know how much," she told the class, silently thanking God for their forgiving spirit.

*Forgive us, Lord, when we get so busy and tired
we don't reflect You.*

9

LAST DAY OF SCHOOL

Frank Pritchard faced the last day of school with mingled emotions. How much had he really taught his lively students in the last nine months? He sat down at his desk and reached for the bell to call the class to order. "What...?" A large bow-topped package with the mysterious inscription OPEN BEFORE STUDENTS LEAVE sat before him. Curious, he lifted the lid and peered at the brightly painted wooden apples. Each had been painstakingly tagged with a student's name.

On top lay a note from a room mother. "Mr. Pritchard, you have planted a seed in each child. Your teachings will sprout and some-day become strong trees. Thank you."

SEEDS

May we never cease
to plant tiny seeds of knowledge
that they may someday
produce abundant fruit.

Thank You, Lord, for strength to keep planting.

THE BRIDGE-BUILDER

An old man, going a lone highway
Came at the evening, cold and gray,
To a chasm vast and wide and steep,
With waters rolling cold and deep.
The old man crossed in the twilight dim;
The sullen stream had no fears for him.
But he turned when safe on the other side,
And built a bridge to span the tide.

"Old man," said a fellow pilgrim near,
"You are wasting your strength with building here.
Your journey will end with the ending day,
You never again will pass this way.
You've crossed the chasm, deep and wide,
Why build you this bridge at eventide?"
The builder lifted his old gray head.

 Apples for A Teacher

"Good friend, in the path I have come," he said,
"There followed after me today
A youth whose feet must pass this way.
The chasm that was as naught to me
To that fair-haired youth may a pitfall be;
He, too, must cross in the twilight dim—
Good friend, I am building this bridge for him."

WILL ALLEN DROMGOOLE (1860-1934)

*Father, help me to build strong bridges and to prepare my students
for the chasms "vast and wide and steep" they must face
throughout their lives.*

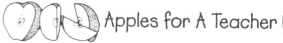 

MICHAEL

Mrs. Ames looked at the new boy in her class and sighed. No matter what she did, she couldn't seem to get through to Michael. He simply refused to speak. At times she thought she saw liking in his dark gaze, but his eyes shifted elsewhere when he noticed her watching him. A silent prayer winged up from Mrs. Ames's heart. *It can't be easy for him, coming to a new school this late in this year, Lord, please, help me to reach him.*

Days passed, and nothing happened. Then one afternoon Michael lingered after the others had left for the day. He choked out, "You're all right, Mrs. Ames," then grabbed his books and headed for the door as if ashamed of having spoken.

"Thank you, Michael," she called. He didn't answer. This time it didn't matter.

Thank You, Lord, for answered prayers.

Apples for A Teacher

A TEACHER'S PRAYER

One day I would like
to teach a few people
many wonderful
and beautiful things
that will help them
when they
will one day
teach a few people.

AUTHOR UNKNOWN

*A prayer in its simplest definition is merely a wish
turned God-ward.*

PHILLIPS BROOKS

(Phillips Brooks (1835-1893), is best remembered for the
Christmas carol, "O Little Town of Bethlehem.")

THE ABSOLUTE BEST

Robert Browning wrote, "My business is not to remake myself, but to make the absolute best of what God made."

Teachers are likewise called. Not to remake students, but to help them become the absolute best that God intended.

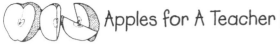 Apples for A Teacher

MAKING A DIFFERENCE

Train a child in the way he should go,
and when he is old he will not turn from it.
PROVERBS 22:6, NIV

Leitha Rensink loved young people second only to God and her family. Every Sunday morning she announced in class, "Be sure to come to Thursday night Young People's Meeting. We're going to have something we've never had before." (Everyone in the church and half the teenagers in town, regardless of their church denomination, came to Young People's Meeting.) If at times Leitha grew discouraged and wondered whether she had made a difference, no one ever knew but God.

Years later she received a letter that she would treasure forever. Enclosed was a published article telling how one of her former students now taught Sunday school and youth classes. Leitha's wonderful examples and lessons of twenty years before were alive and well!

Note: I was the teenager, the teacher, the author, whose life was so richly blessed by the ministry of my dedicated teacher/youth leader. C. L. R.

THE SCULPTOR

I took a piece of plastic clay
And idly fashioned it one day,
And as my fingers pressed it, still
It bent and yielded to my will.

I came again, when days were passed,
The bit of clay was hard at last.
The form I gave it, still it bore,
But I could change that form no more.

 Apples for A Teacher

I took a piece of *living* clay
And gently formed it, day by day
And molded with my power and art
A young child's soft and yielding heart.

I came again when years were gone,
It was a man I looked upon.
He still that early impress bore,
And I could change it, nevermore.

AUTHOR UNKNOWN

Dear Lord, guide my stumbling words and fingers
as I help to mold young lives.

EVERY CHILD

Every child needs a climbing tree
With branches spread invitingly.
Every child needs a cozy bed,
Pillows soft for a nodding head.
Every child needs strong arms, warm,
Encircling, to keep out harm.
Not all children have climbing trees,
A cozy bed or security.
What common bond do children share?
Our Father's love, His endless care.

Father, help me reflect Your love and care to every child
who enters my life.

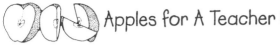 Apples for A Teacher

AS A GIRL THINKS, SO IS SHE

As he thinketh in his heart, so is he.
PROVERBS 23:7, KJV

Jolene, a victim of child abuse, had recently been placed in a foster home. Now as she stared blankly out the classroom window, her teacher became more concerned. Jolene was exhibiting the unmistakable signs of depression.

One day after class Jolene confessed to Mr. Wilson that she felt worthless and that everything must be her fault. He just listened.

The next day he wrote on the board in large block letters, AS A MAN THINKS, SO IS HE. He handed each student several sheets of paper. "We are going to start keeping journals. During the next month I want you to write two things every day: something you did that day you liked—no matter how small—and something you felt good about."

The first few days Jolene struggled. Yet soon her self-esteem improved. Her depression vanished. On the last day of the month she smiled and showed Mr. Wilson something special: a new journal ready for the next month. On the cover she had written, AS A GIRL THINKS, SO IS SHE.

A PRAYER FOR WISDOM

How can I best touch the lives of my students? How can I establish the right atmosphere for learning? These young children, no matter what their ages, are fragile, and pliable, in my hands. What I say and do can stay with them for a lifetime.

The thought of such power is frightening. I must always remember there is a time to challenge, and a time to let up. A time to scold, and a time to praise. A time to talk, and a time to listen. I long to set my students up for success instead of failure; I strive to build self-confidence and self-esteem rather than frustration.

I need to give my best on both good days and bad, through vigor and exhaustion. I need my students' forgiveness when I err. Help me forgive them when they make mistakes. Lord, give me wisdom, strength, and sensitivity. And please, God, help me never to give up.

In Jesus' name, Amen.

A TIME FOR LAUGHTER

My teacher mother entered her classroom every day with joy. She made the most daunting tasks—teaching all eight grades in a one-room school while facing eighth graders far taller than she—seem like child's play. Mom attributed much of her success in teaching three generations of some families to her willingness to laugh.

Experiences from our family vacations in the southwestern United States enlivened her lessons in history and geography. One day she told of the horned toad, a curious desert lizard that spurts tiny streams of blood from its eyes when disturbed. The next day she asked if the class remembered the lizard's odd name.

Dan furiously waved his hand, something he didn't often do. "I know, Mrs. Reece," he shouted. "It's a torn hoad!"

Mom fought back laughter. "Almost, Dan. It's actually a horned toad, but my, you came close!" Her kindness paid off. Dan beamed as brightly as if he'd answered the question perfectly.

MAKING A DIFFERENCE

"**W**e're a family again," Andrea's mother told Mr. Barnes, her voice breaking. "We can never thank you enough." She looked around the classroom. "If it hadn't been for your caring, I don't know what would have happened."

Mr. Barnes blinked hard. He thought how his student had turned to him for help. Andrea's mom was destroying herself and her family with alcohol abuse. "There's nothing we can do," Andrea sobbed.

"Yes, there is," Mr. Barnes insisted. He began praying for them. He encouraged Andrea to get into Alateen, a branch of Alcoholics Anonymous formed to help teenagers with alcoholic parents. Then he accompanied Andrea's father to Al-Anon meetings for family members and friends of alcoholics.

Andrea's mother finally entered the AA program. She had just successfully completed her course. The joy in Andrea's face reflected in her teacher's heart.

FACTS AND FIGURES

A certain elementary principal was asked to pick his all-time outstanding teacher. To the surprise of many, he by-passed eminently qualified teachers, bright and shining stars in the firmament of education. His choice? A white-haired, young-at-heart grandmother who joined in playground games although nearing retirement.

When asked to explain his choice, the principal's eyes took on a faraway look. He said quietly, "Many are excellent teachers of subject material of facts and figures, but Pearl teaches *students*. She makes a difference in their lives."

Dear Lord, help me to teach more than what is in my curriculum.

ANDREW

The Bible is filled with stories of those who never achieved more than second chair in God's orchestra of life. One of the most overshadowed is Andrew, brother of Simon Peter.

"We have found the Messiah!" he shouts on one occasion to Peter and urges his brother to come and see for himself.

Later when Andrew tells Jesus, "There is a small boy with five barley loaves and two little fishes," Jesus increases the child's lunch a thousandfold and more.

When God passes out the "well-done-thou-good-and-faithful-servant" awards, the Andrews among us may very well receive the choicest blessings for their quiet and often unrecognized service.

ANOTHER ANDREW

Andrew was a dreamer. Instead of doing schoolwork, his six-year-old attention strayed out the window to the cloud formations or to flowers on his teacher's desk. "May we stop working and draw some pretty flowers?" he often pleaded.

One afternoon Andrew's class ran relay races on the playground. Andrew and a girl brought up the end of each line. Their turns came and Andrew sprinted ahead. Cheers rose, especially from the boy's teacher who stood at the finish line. Surely, his team would win!

Halfway through the race Andrew stopped. To everyone's amazement, he bent down and picked a flower. Then he slowly walked to his teacher, smelled the flower, and held it out to her with a delightful, loving smile.

The next day each first-grader received a large piece of drawing paper to make whatever they wished. The room hummed with content.

Andrew drew a flower.

Father, help me appreciate the "specialness" of every child.

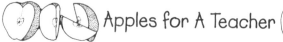 

BEING THERE

Seventeen and pregnant, with the baby's father too immature to accept any responsibility, Rayanna sought out her favorite teacher.

"I'll always be here for you," Mrs. Snyder promised. She listened as Rayanna expressed fear and considered options concerning her unborn child. Many times she gave up most of her lunch break, or scheduled meetings with Rayanna after school. Sometimes she sighed that she had so little time for herself, but she kept on being there.

Rayanna stayed with her parents and kept her baby. Even after she graduated from high school, she managed to keep in contact with her teacher. Two years later Mrs. Snyder watched Rayanna walk across the stage and receive her Associate of Arts degree in book-keeping. After the ceremony Rayanna handed her teacher a gradua-tion card. Inside was written, "Thank you. I love you. I could never have done it without you."

Mrs. Snyder knew at that moment she also had just graduated.

A word fitly spoken is like apples of gold in pictures of silver.
PROVERBS 25:11, KJV

"YOU CAN DO IT"

Thirteen-year-old Jennifer was a proverbial square peg in a round hole. Fellow students teased her unmercifully, yet she decided to turn out for track. Marcy, the coach, felt drawn to the lonely girl from the start. She longed for Jennifer to do her best. Every day at practice she drilled into her, "You have the makings of a winner. You can do it." Jennifer practiced hard.

On the day of the track meet no one paid much attention when Jennifer was up to run the mile. Then someone pointed across the field. Legs working like well-oiled pistons, Jennifer surged ahead of the others—and won! Other successes followed until Jennifer went on to the state competition and did well.

Those few little words, "You can do it," had created a winner.

*Dear Lord, help me never to be so busy I fail to encourage,
especially those who silently cry out for my help
and can do great things if someone believes in them.*

One thing I do: Forgetting what is behind...I press on....
PHILIPPIANS 3:13-14, NIV

 Apples for A Teacher

DOING THE IMPOSSIBLE

Mrs. Towne stepped into a strangely quiet junior high class. Thirty-five pairs of eyes stared at her.

She didn't flinch. "I understand you had trouble with your former teacher." In fact, Miss Jones had been literally forced out of the classroom after several unpleasant incidents, ending with her slapping a boy's face.

Outraged cries detailed the list of indignities Miss Jones had dealt the class.

Mrs. Towne raised her hand. "I'm not here to judge either you or Miss Jones. But I will say this. In spite of everything, when she was ready to leave she asked me to tell you she loved you all. Now, what's past is past. Let's go from here."

Mrs. Towne never had a problem. Years later even the biggest boys in that class came to see her and proclaimed her the best teacher they'd ever had.

 Apples for A Teacher

"IT COULDN'T BE DONE"

Have you ever dreaded having a certain student in your class because of negative advance publicity? You might have felt you were beaten before you got started.

Edgar A. Guest in his poem, "It Couldn't be Done" tells of a man who *wouldn't* buy into this philosophy.

A certain junior high creative writing teacher also swam against the tide. She saw talent in a boy who loved to pretend all through his younger years. He hated structured tasks, seemed disorganized, and showed little promise. The teacher turned the boy loose to write, and write, and write. He went on to college and wrote some more.

One day his former teacher received a short note. "You are invited to the opening night of my first play. Complimentary tickets await you at the door. Perhaps you'll bring a student who loves to write as much as I do. Thank you for believing in me when no one else—including myself—did."

*Father, help me to remember the choicest laurel wreaths
are the hardest won.*

PRAYER

Lord, make me an instrument of Thy peace.
Where there is hatred, let me sow love.
Where there is injury, pardon.
Where there is doubt, faith.
Where there is despair, hope.
Where there is darkness, light.
Where there is sadness, joy.

ST. FRANCIS OF ASSISI

 Apples for A Teacher

SILVER SPOON KIDS

*S*ome teachers have problems with troublemakers or under-achievers. Not Mrs. Harden. The children who set her teeth on edge were, as she called them, "silver spoon kids," snobbish, spoiled children who have everything they want and more.

Alexandra was such a kid. Mrs. Harden disliked her from the first day of school. Every time she asked Alexandra to complete a difficult assignment, the girl either pouted or whined.

"I have to change my attitude," Mrs. Harden confessed. "If Alexandra senses my feelings, I'll never get through to her." She began to see how insecure and unhappy Alexandra was. Everything had been done for her.

The conscientious teacher worked hard at building self-esteem. A few months later Alexandra blossomed into an energetic, bubbly, friendly child who gave of herself to others. She was even named classroom student of the month!

Mrs. Harden felt even more pleased than her student.

Free me from prejudice, Lord, that I may serve.

YOU MUST DECIDE...

Mrs. Randall prepared carefully for her fourth-grade science class. She had prayed at length about how to teach the difficult lesson on how the earth and people began. After presenting the theories in the science book, she concluded, "And some people believe God created everything."

A student raised his hand. "I don't believe we just happened. I think God made us."

Mrs. Randall quietly allowed the class to discuss their views. Finally one student demanded, "What do you think, teacher?"

"I believe God made this earth and us, but you must decide for yourselves."

The class continued their discussion and decided the same thing.

Thank You, Lord, for teaching these young minds, Mrs. Randall silently prayed.

THE RIGHT WORDS

A word fitly spoken is like apples of gold in pictures of silver.
PROVERBS 25:11, KJV

"How big is God?" Primary Sunday school student Shawn asked his teacher.

The teacher chuckled. "To find that answer, I want you to go home and do three things: measure how big the sky is, how deep the ocean is, and how far you would go if you traveled around the world seven times."

Shawn pondered those measurements all week. The next Sunday he told his teacher, "It's too big to figure out." He sighed.

The teacher smiled. "Shawn, all I want you to know is this: God is a lot bigger than anything."

A POINT TO PONDER
AGAIN AND AGAIN

Have I taught for lo, these many years,
or have I only taught one year many times?

*Dear God, save me from trodding a rut of my own making
and give me the desire to bring freshness
and new life to my work.*

 Apples for A Teacher

A LOT OF HARD WORK

Seventeen-year-old Jamie had a learning disability. She wanted to do something special with her life but she was afraid to try.

Mr. Parker listened intently to her concerns. Then he gave her a pep talk. He pointed out that, with hard work, many persons with learning disabilities succeed. Some even have become famous. Some go to college. A few have become teachers.

That's all it took for Jamie. College became her first goal.

Years later an attractive young woman stepped into Mr. Parker's classroom. She shared how she'd just been hired for her first job—teaching first grade special education.

"You were right, Mr. Parker," Jamie admitted, shaking his hand. "It took a lot of hard work but I'm glad I tried. I hope someday I can encourage others as you did me."

EXPECTING THE BEST

My mother ruled her classroom with a rod of love. Insteading of sending students to the office, she handled problems in her own unique manner. One time when she noticed a third-grader surreptitiously copying test answers with a grimy hand, she said nothing.

The next day Mom told the class, "One of the other teachers mentioned that some students in her class were cheating. Isn't that sad? My goodness, we'd *never* do anything like that, would we?"

"Oh, no, Mrs. Reece," her class chorused. The culprit's face turned scarlet and he ducked his head. Her method proved effective. Her sharp gaze never again caught anyone cheating.

A soft answer turneth away wrath:
but grievous words stir up anger.
PROVERBS 15:1, KJV

 Apples for A Teacher

HELP!

Edna loved having her class in the "portable," a one-room building used when an increase in fifth-grade enrollment required another class. The semi-isolation gave added freedom. It also brought surprising results.

One warm afternoon the class sat enthralled. They were reading about how the early settlers in America sometimes got along with the Indians and at other times fought with them. Red-haired Billy sat next to the open window. In the middle of the most exciting part, a hand reached in, grabbed his hair, and pulled.

He rose out of his seat yelling, "Help, I'm being scalped!"

The grinning face of a high school boy on his way to the ball field appeared in the window. "Sorry," he gasped between laughing. "I heard your story and couldn't resist."

Thank You, Father, for the gift of laughter
that brightens our days.

ONE SOLITARY LIFE

He was born in an obscure village, the child of a peasant woman. He worked in a carpenter shop until He was thirty, then became an itinerant preacher. He never wrote a book. He never held an office. He never did one thing that usually accompanies greatness. He had no credentials but Himself. While still a young man, public opinion turned against Him. His friends ran away. One denied Him. He went through the mockery of a trial. He was nailed to a cross between two thieves. His executioners gambled for His only piece of property—His coat. He was laid in a borrowed grave.

Nineteen wide centuries have come and gone. Today He is the centerpiece of the human race. All the armies that ever marched, all the navies that ever sailed, all the parliaments that ever sat, and all the kings that ever reigned put together, have not affected the life of man upon this earth as powerfully as that One Solitary Life.

AUTHOR UNKNOWN

ONE BOY

He was an average, quiet boy who seldom stood out in school. He loved drawing, and specialized in airplanes. After he finished his schoolwork, he filled page after page with his pictures of airplanes. Teachers accommodated his drawings but no one made much of them. His dreams clearly were in the stars.

The boy grew into manhood. He joined the Air Force and years later literally traveled to the stars.

His name? Astronaut Dick Scobee, Mission Commander of the space shuttle *Challenger.*

> *God, keep reminding me that You have planted seeds*
> *of greatness in humble persons.*

HOLD HIGH THE TORCH

Hold high the torch!
You did not light its glow—
'Twas given you by other hands, you know.
'Tis yours to keep it burning bright,
Yours to pass on when you no more need light.
For there are other feet that we must guide,
And other forms go marching by our sides.
Their eyes are watching every smile and tear,
And efforts that we think are not worthwhile
Are sometimes just the very help they need,
So that in turn they'll hold it high and say,
"I watched someone else carry it this way."

Apples for A Teacher

Hold high the torch!
You did not light its glow—
'Twas given you by other hands, you know.
I think it started down its pathway bright
The day the Maker said, "Let there be light."
And He once said, who hung on Calvary's tree—
"Ye are the light of the world ...Go!...Shine—for Me."

AUTHOR UNKNOWN

Lord, thank You for calling me to carry the torch of learning.
Help me to hold it high, so its—and Your—light might spread
into dark corners, banishing ignorance, prejudice, and fear.

PERFECTLY BEAUTIFUL

*C*risp air. Multicolored leaves. Time to make a much-loved project—mobiles, color-splashed with a variety of leaves gathered by students. Pressed between layers of waxed paper, they hung in artistic balance above the students' desks.

One afternoon Andrea slammed down her pencil. She was in tears at her failure to do perfect work. Her teacher took down her own mobile and showed the pressed leaves to the class. "Are any the same?" she asked. "Look at the tear in this one, the brown spots on another. How about this leaf where a caterpillar ate through the middle? Aren't they all beautiful?"

The students nodded. Their teacher carefully slipped one leaf off and placed it in Andrea's hand. "Remember, things don't have to be perfect to be good. Turn the leaf over. You can also turn your leaf of paper over and start again."

Andrea glanced at her own mobile often. It became a reminder for her to relax, to enjoy her work, and not to worry so much about being perfect.

 Apples for A Teacher

THERE WAS A LITTLE GIRL

There was a little girl, who had a little curl
Right in the middle of her forehead;
And when she was good, she was very, very good,
And when she was bad, she was horrid.

HENRY WADSWORTH LONGFELLOW

When kindness, discipline, and even love fail to reach troubled, even horrid-acting children, teachers still have the most powerful weapon of all: prayer.

Alfred, Lord Tennyson wrote, "More things are wrought by prayer than this world dreams of. Wherefore, let thy voice rise like a fountain...night and day."

Father, help me to pray unceasingly.

TWICE LOVED

Kevin angrily kicked a pebble across the play area. *Oh, no,* special education teacher Angela Garman thought. *Another bad day.* His second-grade teacher reported Kevin just wasn't making progress socially.

Angela's attention was then diverted to one of her own students.

Marcy obviously wanted to play with the other children, but she didn't know how to make friends. Angela sighed. That night she wondered how to help. A Bible verse seemed to tug at her mind: "A little child shall lead them" (Isaiah 11:6, KJV).

The next day she approached Kevin's teacher. Their discussion resulted in the second graders "adopting" Angela's special ed children, and Kevin chose Marcy. Day after day he talked to her, held her hand, and coaxed her into playing games. Finally, during recess, she called out, "Kewin, wait up!" She happily raced toward her new friend, dark curls bouncing.

Kevin also changed. He told Angela, "Marcy is my friend. She needs me. I said a prayer for her. Do you think she's a secret little angel?"

"Yes, Kevin." Angela blinked and thanked God for love shared twice by two wonderful children.

 Apples for A Teacher

STILL LOVED

S pecial education teacher Angela Garman purposely sat near the aisle in the back of the large room. High school graduation: one she wouldn't miss for anything.

Eighteen-year-old Kevin stood a lanky, handsome six-foot, four on his special day. He flashed Angela a nervous smile. The graduates were lining up to enter.

Then a rustle was heard near the back of the line. "Wait up, Kevin."

Marcy hurried to Kevin's side and smiled up at him. Her long, dark hair still hung in luxurious ringlets.

Kevin straightened Marcy's tassel and grinned back. "You'll always be my buddy, Marcy. Let's go." He gallantly raised his arm toward her.

Angela felt a tear trickle down her cheek as she watched two old friends start down the aisle to receive their diplomas.

Thank You, Lord, for the gift of childhood friendships
that can last a lifetime.

GIFT FROM THE HEART

First-grader Jennifer's parents were struggling financially. She didn't have many nice things, but she did have a favorite rag doll. She brought her worn doll with yellow yarn hair that matched her own to school at least once a week. At Christmastime her eyes sparkled as she watched her teacher open a package with a wrinkled red bow.

"Why, Jennifer," Mrs. McKenzie stammered as she held the rag doll. "I can't accept this."

Jennifer's smile died. She ran to her desk and buried her face in her arms.

The teacher called Jennifer's mother immediately. She learned the little girl loved her teacher so much she wanted to give a gift from the heart.

Mrs. McKenzie went back to her classroom and straight to Jennifer. "You're sure you want me to have her?"

Jennifer nodded.

"I'll always treasure her," her teacher whispered. She hugged Jennifer then placed the doll on a shelf for all to see.

Years later Mrs. McKenzie retired. But Jennifer's doll always had a special place on a shelf in her home.

REMINDER GIFT

Robert had let too many things pile up on his school holiday agenda. He gripped his pen until his knuckles turned white. *One more change in the Christmas program.* "I hope that makes people happy," he muttered. "I hate all this petty jealousy and nit-picking over trivial things. At least it's not my fault."

His students burst through the door, taking away what little peace of mind he had left.

One small girl stood by his desk. "Mr. Morris, I have a s'prise for you." She held out a nativity so tiny it fit in the palm of her hand. Robert gazed into baby Jesus' face, and suddenly the true meaning of the "school holiday" became clear. "Thank you, Susan," he whispered.

Thank You, God, for giving me simple reminders of Your love when I need them most.

TASAPIO

"**H**ey, Mrs. D., I like your frog." Dustin lightly touched the bumpy head of the life-sized ceramic frog on my desk. The frog appeared to be looking up at Dustin with a big grin. I used the green critter to help students develop self-esteem.

"What's his name?"

"Tasapio."

"Tah-sap-ee-o? That's a funny name for a frog."

"It's short for Take A Smile And Pass It On."

"Cool!" he exclaimed, nodding.

Others thought so, too. Tasapio became our class password. When someone looks a little down, I still hear the word "Tasapio." Students break out in a grin—and sometimes even say it to me!

ONE FLOWER

"**I** can't believe Mom lately," Shelly fumed. "She's so hard to get along with. She expects me to jump through all the hoops just because my sixteenth birthday is coming up."

"This is a special day for her, as well as for you," her teacher Doris soothed. "Want to know how to stop the arguing?"

"Sure."

"Go buy her a flower."

"Excuse me?" Shelly looked astonished.

"Go buy her one flower."

Shelly did. The next day she thanked her teacher.

Doris chuckled and flipped open the front cover of her dictionary. There lay a pressed rose with a note: "To Mom, with love."

Thank You for the healing possibilities of one flower, Lord.

FROM "GRADATIM"

Heaven is not gained at a single bound;
But we build the ladder by which we rise
From the lowly earth to the vaulted skies,
And we mount to its summit, round by round.

JOSIAH GILBERT HOLLAND

Each new school year or Sunday school class we begin is like a ladder. We start at the bottom, filled with high expectations, aspirations, and dreams of the glorious view from the top. Yet we mount the ladder rung by rung. Some students forge ahead. Others lag behind.

We have our reward in the lives of those students who achieve the top of the ladder. Yet, in the sight of the Master Teacher, the help we give to those who struggle with every step upward may well be far more precious.

 Apples for A Teacher

JULIE

*J*ulie, a developmentally delayed six year old, bounced into class on her first day of school. Her records told Miss Hodson that Julie could neither talk nor sign with her fingers; she would probably never be able to speak.

Day after day Julie and her teacher played learning games. The little girl's carrot-colored pony tail flipped to the rhythm of her infectious giggle. Every day Miss Hodson ended the same way. "Hug for Julie. I'm proud of you."

Months passed. Julie learned several sign language words but never spoke. Miss Hodson quietly kept praying.

One afternoon when she took Julie to the bus, a tinkly voice rose above those of the chattering students. "Hug!"

Miss Hodson froze and glanced down at Julie's outstretched arms. "Hug."

The teacher bent down. "Hug, Julie. I'm very proud of you," she whispered.

Miss Hodson waved until the bus drove out of sight. *Thanks, Lord. It's only the beginning.*

WINGS OF EAGLES

The car accident happened so fast Mark couldn't even recall the events. Now as he lay in his hospital bed, Mark, a gifted athlete, wondered if he would ever walk again, let alone run. Fear washed over him. He shoved it aside when his Sunday school teacher came in for a visit.

Ken pulled a poster from a sack and handed it to Mark. The boy unfolded it. "All right!" He stared at the huge eagle, its mighty wings spread in flight, and the Scripture at the bottom.

"You can do it, Mark," Ken said. "This may be the biggest hurdle you ever have to clear. With God's help, *you can do it*."

In the following weeks and months Mark traced the eagle's wings with his fingers a hundred times. He prayed for help as he sweated and struggled to regain the use of his legs.

Two years later, Mark won his high school track meet hurdles race. Ken met him at the finish line. Mark threw his arms around his Sunday school teacher. "One more hurdle," he said, panting. Ken just hugged him.

 Apples for A Teacher

THE SCRIPTURE
ON THE POSTER

But they that wait upon the LORD shall renew their strength; they shall mount up with wings as eagles; they shall run, and not be weary; and they shall walk, and not faint.
ISAIAH 40:31, KJV

WORTH CONSIDERING

But they that wait upon the LORD shall renew their strength;
they shall mount up with wings as eagles; they shall run,
and not be weary; and they shall walk, and not faint.
ISAIAH 40:31, KJV

Most people who read this Scripture consider waiting upon the Lord to mean pausing, lingering, tarrying. A second meaning may be equally or even more applicable: waiting upon the Lord as in serving Him.

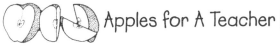 

EULOGY FOR A TEACHER

How will you be remembered
By those who come to you?
What will they say,
The ones you serve,
When teaching days are through?

"He never had a favorite."
"He smiled when he was down."
"She made me feel that I was loved."
All jewels in your crown.

And yet one priceless accolade
Out-sparkles all the rest.
A single phrase sums up the days:
"My teacher gave his best."

GIVING

*"Self-sacrifice is the real miracle out of which all
the reported miracles grow."*

RALPH WALDO EMERSON

Belinda and her family had faced numerous tragedies in the past year, including death in the family and her husband's serious illness and inability to work. In order to make it financially, Belinda had to take on two jobs.

Joanne, her adult Sunday school teacher, kept in touch and offered a listening ear. The class took up a love offering and Joanne delivered it Christmas Eve. After hugs and tears the Sunday school teacher reached into her purse and took out one more thing, a shiny ornament in the shape of a small light bulb. Its bright coating reflected the light in the room.

Joanne said, "Keep smiling. With God's help, there's always light ahead."

The ornament hangs in Belinda's kitchen window year after year. Its spinning reflection helps her remember God's care, and she continues to rejoice over victories won in her family.

 Apples for A Teacher

OVERLOAD

*C*andice hated being chubby. At fifteen looking thin meant everything. She starved to take off pounds, then missed class due to fatigue, stomach cramps, and mood swings.

Sandra Martin was Candice's counselor. "How's the diet going?" she inquired one afternoon.

"Terrible." Candice slumped against her locker.

"I just started a diet where you eat good foods, lose weight, and still feel great. Want to try it?"

"I only lose by starving. Besides, no one cares if I get sick."

"I care. Let's do it together." At that moment, Sandra had an inspiration. "I could use another peer counselor. Would you be interested?"

"The kids will think I'm fat and ugly," Candice protested, but her eyes shone.

"Give them a break, will you? They have problems, too."

Candice and her teacher kept so busy helping others, neither had time to sit around and munch on snacks. Both lost weight and Candice found a new dream: counseling.

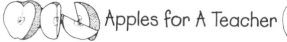 

THE MASTER'S HAND

Myra Brooks Welch's poem, "The Touch of the Master's Hand," tells how an auctioneer held up a battered violin and called for a bid. Just when he was ready to sell it for $3.00, a master violinist stepped forward and played the most beautiful song imaginable. The violin sold for $3,000. The touch of the master's hand had changed the instrument's worth.

The poem contains an analogy of how many persons are auctioned off cheaply, but when the Master steps in, their lives are changed forever.

Father, when I am frustrated and wonder if what I do is worth anything, help me to remember how precious I am to You and to others.

BURNT TOAST

Seven A.M. Running late, Cheryl had wanted to be at school an hour early to finish a pile of work. Now as she trimmed the blackened edges of her toast, something inside nudged her to take time for a quick devotion. She opened her Bible and grinned. "To every thing there is a season, and a time to every purpose under the heaven" (Ecclesiastes 3:1, KJV).

"Great sense of humor, God," she muttered. "There's a time, all right, even for burnt toast. Please, don't let this day be like my breakfast."

That morning Mark had trouble with his reading. Cheryl patted his shoulder. "Come on, Mark. I'll help you. It's like trimming the edges off burnt toast. We'll get rid of the hard stuff first, and the rest will be all right."

God's timing was perfect, as always.

A TRIBUTE GIVEN

She was outspoken and firm. She never minced words. Her classroom hummed with her students' diligent work. She ran a tight ship, but warmth and caring accompanied her firm ways. Her door always stood open before school, should anyone want to slip in for extra help or just to study quietly.

Her class discussions had me sitting on the edge of my seat. She inspired me to write my first story. Though conservative with her "A's" she gave me one for the story and the year. She recognized potential in me I didn't know existed.

Lydia Case, my beloved eleventh-grade English teacher, lit my candle to write. She left me with the philosophy, "Never settle for *your* second best."

Thank you, Lydia Case.

ANITA (HATCH) DONIHUE

A TRIBUTE RECEIVED

One of the most humbling incidents in my life happened when a well-known children's author came to me. "I've wanted to tell you this for years," she began. "Colleen, you changed my life."

I stared and listened.

At a writers' conference years before one editor's decision had almost shattered her hopes and dreams. As she prepared to leave, a fellow staff member saw her stricken face and brought her to a class I was teaching for beginners. I shared my ups and downs as well as what I'd learned along the rocky road to authorship. She got excited and realized the rejection of even the most precious manuscript isn't the end of the world. She left the conference feeling that she *had* been called to write and determined to do whatever it took to succeed.

Father, may we as teachers not only be instruments in Thy hands, but shining tools You can use for Your best purposes.

 Apples for A Teacher

LITTLE THINGS

Dan's classroom and coaching duties kept him pretty busy, but he couldn't help noticing how stressed the school principal seemed. Mr. Markworth had kicked into high gear to get ready for the upcoming science fair. With every passing day he looked more worn. His usual smile had vanished with only a grimace to replace it.

What can I do? Dan wondered. *I'm only a teacher. I don't know anything about keeping a finger on the pulse of the whole school the way he does.* Dan prayed, but he wished he could do more. Then an idea came to him. On a piece of paper he wrote these words: *Just a note to say thanks for being a great principal. You are appreciated more than you know. Let me know if*—he hesitated, crossing the last word out—*how I can help.* Dan scrawled his name and dropped the note in the principal's mailbox.

The next time Dan saw Mr. Markworth, the principal approached him eagerly. "Thanks. Everything's finally under control, but your note really helped. Funny how little things really do make a difference." He walked away smiling.

Lord, help me to remember the importance of "little things."

Presented to

_____

On the occasion of

_____

From

_____

Date

_____

Published by Barbour Publishing, Inc., P.O. Box 719, Uhrichsville, Ohio 44683
http://www.barbourbooks.com

Member of the
Evangelical Christian
Publishers Association

Printed in China.

101 WAYS TO SAY

I Love You

BARBOUR
PUBLISHING, INC.

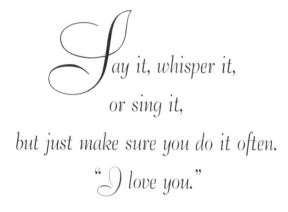

Say it, whisper it,
or sing it,
but just make sure you do it often.
"I love you."

2
Send flowers.
From the florist or your garden,
the essence
is the same.

3
Send poetry.
From the pen of Solomon,
Elizabeth Barrett Browning, or you,
the meaning is the same.

4
Say "Will you marry me?"
You might light up the scoreboard at the stadium. . .

5

Or, proclaim your intentions on a high-flying banner
(pulled by an airplane) at the beach. . .

6

Or, broadcast your desires on tape,
spliced over a commercial
on one of her favorite prerecorded romantic movies. . .

7

Or, pop the question
after a treasure hunt of sorts,
with the diamond of her dreams carefully concealed.

8

Or, propose over a candlelight dinner at the scene of
your first date or meeting, including
an empty football stadium,
a deserted beach,
an airplane hangar—
almost anywhere.

9

Paddle your love through moonlit waters.

10

Give a gift for no reason,
except to say "I love you."

11
Compliment the love of your life often,
in private and in public.

12
Hide little gifts around the house
for your spouse.

13
Write a note to your spouse, then hide it in a special,
sure-to-be-found place.

14
Send a love note by overnight delivery.
(Write: "I just couldn't wait to say 'I love you.'")

15
Give big bear hugs.

16
Sit next to your wife
in the restaurant booth,
not across from her.

17

Spend time with the one you love. Share a simple lunch,
play board games, take a walk, go for a
bike ride (tandem, too).

18

Suggest activities you know
your spouse will enjoy
(even if you'd rather do something else).

19

Spend the first fifteen minutes upon arriving home
each day visiting with your spouse. Alone.

20

Treat your love to a triple-scoop ice cream cone.

21

Plan a weekend fishing or
camping trip with your spouse.
It's a chance to be together without
interruption. . .a chance
to recapture intimacy.

22

Surprise your spouse. Make the bed,
do the dishes, go grocery shopping,
shovel the sidewalk, balance the checkbook,
pick up the dry cleaning. . .
make your own love list.

Give lingering kisses.

24
Plan a night or a weekend
at a charming bed and breakfast inn
with your spouse.

25
Tie on that apron
and give your spouse a night off in the kitchen.

26
Sew on buttons for your
husband.

27

Wash each other's cars on a
hot summer day.
(Chase each other with the hose.)

28

Perfect your bedside manner.
Put together a care package by filling a cookie tin
with soup mix, cold tablets, throat lozenges, magazines,
and maybe a really good chocolate bar.
Tie a bright bow around it and seal with a kiss.
(The real thing will be a reward for recovery.)

29
Rent a convertible
on a beautiful summer day
and drive to the beach.

30
Start a devotional time for
just the two of you.

31
Read old love letters
(from each other!) together.

32
Walk hand in hand on a beach
at sunset. And then have a
cookout on the sand.

33
Plan a "mystery night" once a month.
Secret destinations might include
a concert, favorite or new restaurant,
or weekend getaway. Keep all the
arrangements to yourself
as long as possible
(although guessing is fun, too).

34
Re-create your first date
together.

35
Watch the sunrise together.
And then go out for breakfast.

36
Tour country roads together, by bike,
car, or horseback.
Take along a picnic lunch
(and a camera).

37
Give your chosen one a book by
a favorite author. Romantically inscribe the first page
(be sure to include the date).

Rent an old movie to watch together on a chilly, rainy day—under a blanket.

39
Create your own holiday
traditions.

40
Surprise your heartthrob with tickets
to his or her favorite team's game.
(Make sure the seats aren't in the
nosebleed section!)

41
Plan a service project together: volunteer
at a homeless shelter, soup kitchen, or
hospital ward. Enrich your own relationship
as you enrich the lives of others.

42
Surprise your sweetheart by
taking him or her out to lunch.

43
Telephone your true love
unexpectedly—"I just called to
say 'I love you.' . . ."

44
Keep a thank-you jar. Throughout the year
jot down reasons why you're thankful
for your spouse and then
read them aloud on your anniversary.

45
Share with your love
your love of Jesus Christ.

46
Encourage each other's hobbies.

47
Give a small gift every day of the week
(or month) preceding a birthday
or anniversary.

48
Lie outside on a blanket
on a clear night
and watch the stars.

49
Slip a love note in his lunch sack.

50
Call a local radio station and dedicate
"your song" to the one you love.

51
Remember your wedding day. Every now and then,
go through your wedding album
or watch your wedding
video together.

52
Remind your spouse why you
love him or her more with every year.

53
Pray for each other.

54
Have a professional photographer
take your portrait. Give yourself (uniquely
framed) to the one you love.

55
Keep a scrapbook
of your life together.

56
Plan a dream vacation.

57

Create special nonverbal signals. Three hand
squeezes might mean "I love you"; rubbing your
chin could say "Let's get out of here!".

58

Write a letter to your future mother-in-law.
Tell her how blessed you
are to marry her child.

59

Escape a dreary Saturday
over cups of cappucino.

60

Write a letter—years later—to your
mother-in-law. Thank her for raising
such a wonderful man to be your husband.

61

Plant a tree together on
your first anniversary
(or when the weather warms up).

62

Learn a new sport together.

63

Learn to play a sport
your significant other
already enjoys.

64

Enroll in a ballroom dancing class.
(There were major sparks, after all,
between Fred and Ginger.)

65

Be the first to make up. Don't let
a day end with an argument.

Remind each other of the reasons you

fell in love.

67

Throw a surprise birthday party
for the one you love.
First, though, make sure they'll
appreciate such a gesture.

68

Make sure you look
your best when you're out
with your spouse.

69

Keep in shape. Chances are, you'll spend more years
with your spouse, and you'll be more attractive
to her or him.

70

Give your bride a day of beauty at a local spa.
(Then pour on the compliments!)

71

Comfort your spouse. Tender is the day
and night when you offer a shoulder to cry on,
a handkerchief
to wipe away the tears.

72

Be a gentleman. Hold open all doors for her,
pull out (and push in) her chair,
introduce her proudly to others.

73
Secure her future. Make out a will
after you're married.

74
Attend church and
Sunday school together.

75
Encourage your spouse to go out with friends.
Every relationship needs some
breathing room.

76
Prepare a gourmet meal together.
(The kitchen is the perfect place for
a "chemistry" lesson.)

77
Go clothes shopping
with your wife.
Insist she try on many outfits.

78
Suggest her or his parents come
for a visit (or for dinner).

79
Share household
responsibilities.

80
Learn to say
"I love you" in a
foreign language.

81
Share babysitting
responsibilities.

82
Speak kindly to (and of)
your spouse—always,
no matter what.

83
Call every day you're away
on a business trip.

84
Call in "well" and spend a weekday together.
Stroll through a favorite museum.
Lunch leisurely at an obscure bistro
which, unlike your love, is a well-kept secret.

85
Hold hands when going
for a walk.

86
Hold on to each other when
the going gets rough.

87
Display at work a photo
of your spouse.

88
Laugh even when your beloved
blows the punchline.

89
Laugh even when you've heard her joke
quite a few times before.

90
Smile when the
woman or man you love
enters the room.

91
Make up your own nicknames
for each other.

92
Celebrate all of your spouse's
accomplishments—big or small—
with panache.

93
Decorate your home with beauty—bright colors,
flowers, music, warmth, and laughter—
and love will always be there.

94
Tape a love note to the
bathroom mirror.

95
Give a shoulder massage after a stressful day
at work or school.

96
Raise your daughter to see in her father
what a husband should be.

97

Remember the love you've shared all year.
Give your spouse a Christmas tree
ornament that brings back a special memory.

98

Raise your son to aspire to win a woman
like his mother.

99

Remember that your marriage vows
were made before God.

100
Retreat at the end of each year to a mountain cabin
(or anywhere away from civilization).
Beside a roaring fire assess the past year
together. Dream dreams
for the year ahead.

101
Return to the place you spent your
honeymoon. Renew your love for each other.